THE UNREASONABLE TRANSFORMERS OF SOUTH INDIA

PUSHPANATH
KRISHNAMURTHY

ISBN
Hardcase 979-8-89906-822-5
Paperback 979-8-89724-966-4

Contents

Acknowledgment – A Handful of Gratitude

There's a proverb I heard often in Malawi, that landlocked but luminous country in the heart of southern Africa—*No single person can hold up the sky*. It is a phrase that stayed with me, wrapped itself around my thoughts, and whispered in my ear as I set out on this journey.

The stories of the **Unreasonable Transformers of South India** might have remained just that—dreams, flickering at the edge of memory—if not for the people who, knowingly or unknowingly, held up the sky for me.

First, my immediate family—Uma, my wife, my anchor. Our sons, Shyam and Ahir, our daughters-in-law, Nisha and Kareen, and our grandchildren, Anir, Rudran, and Reya. They endured my long absences, my self-absorption, my vanishing into words and worlds, yet never wavered in their love and quiet, unflinching support at many levels of this process.

To the supporting organizations and members – WEALL – Simon Ticehurst, Thobile Chittenden and Michael Weatherhead; Non Violent Economy movement(Ahimsa)-Jill Carr-Harriss and Rabbi Dinakaran, Priya Krishnamurthy-200 million artisans.

To my dearest friends—Shiva Prakash, Dr K. Panjaksharan CEO, SIPA, Gopal Rao, and Anil Annaiah—keepers of faith, bearers of light. And to Joe Human, who has been my lodestar, my constant inspiration. Their encouragement, their quiet presence, their belief in this endeavor nudged me forward when doubt came knocking.

At the heart of it all are the **Unreasonable Transformers** themselves—restless, relentless, irrepressible. Their stories, their audacity, their incandescent refusal to accept the way things are. What I have written is but my own rendering of their lives, my own version of how I saw, read, and felt them. This book is theirs as much as it is mine.

And then there were the hands that shaped it in the shadows—the readers who glimpsed these stories in their rawest form, who left behind words of encouragement in drafts, on LinkedIn, on Facebook. Among them, Mariie Banu Rodrigues, whose *Conversations* gave these words a home.

To all of you who, in ways big and small, lifted the sky with me— thank you.

Foreword

It is a privilege to have been asked to write a Forward for Pushpanath Krishnamurthy's forthcoming book "The Unreasonable Transformers in South India". The book is about change-makers in the economic arena, "being stubbornly unreasonable" in order to successfully innovate against the force of the market, 'going against the grain' to integrate sustainability and climate proofing into small businesses, 'thinking out of the box' in order to provide more fairness to the small guy. Pushpanath reminds us that this is not an easy fight: It is requires a force of personality (individual and group) and he shows us many examples of people who have been able to sustain such changes.

The author stories his relationship with these twenty-two change-makers with rich description, many he has known for a long-time. He shows this book as an experiential journey of a narrator like a pilgrimmage, traveling over three months (August to October, 2024) to various artisans' places of work; and he records what he sees in the artful way they combine business and ethical practices with a climate change response. In his intimate portrayal of each change-maker, he exposes their vulnerabilities and yet describes them as heroes (heroines) in an authentic manner. Unlike others who may be good standard bearers of case studies on social businesses, Pushpanath reveals the struggles of survival in a frame of lived experience. His turn of phrases exemplifies this, for instance he speaks of one change maker: "She did not travel in straight lines but in a zigzag of struggle, reinvention and break-though" and this gives the reader the sense of inner determination that is required and as Gandhi said: "to be the change you want to see in the world".

These stories are strung together like a pearl necklace with each shell intimately recounting the purveyors of forest resources for Adivasis people, of different craftspersons, agro-producers of coffee and medicinal herbs, handloom weavers and natural dyers, toy makers, waste management leaders, fashion designers and others. Although his coverage of change-makers was mainly from south India, he did not mean that these did not exist across India. Pushpanath emphasizes the importance of the Kula Conclave a national space for creating interest in India's 200 million artisans to investors. The author shows the importance of Fair Trade India, that builds just trade relationships. He imagines Fair Trade cities. Pushpanath also flags the importance of holding nonviolent marketplaces like the one in Madurai in September 2022 called the Ahimsa Santhai in which 140 producers were able to sell their products directly without dependence on middle-men. The author uses these examples to show that we have to engage the most vulnerable, that it is about justice, not profit. The bottom-line is the author is showing how a nonviolent and sustainable economy already exists in India and that it is for us to build it further.

Pushpanath has demonstrated in his 3-decade long history of promoting just trade, social markets and climate justice how different techniques can be employed like walking on long padyatras across different terrains of different continents; traveling by van and speaking to people in villages, towns and cities; using the social media to press for colourful campaigns – -and in this case story-telling about the heroines of the alternative craft, handloom, food sectors.

In sum, Pushpanath is weaving a tapestry of stories: The warp is the most vulnerable especially women, Adiviasi, minorities, outcastes, and other marginalized communities; the woof is the climate crisis and depleting biodiversity and natural heritage. The weaver has the power to make a change. The book leaves the reader feeling like they too, can be part of the growing number of change-makers that are designing not only a social business but a nonviolent and sustainable economy.

– Jill-Carr-Hariss
Secretary IGINP-International Gndhi Institute
for Nonviolence and Peace,

Message of Strong Support from Weall-Movement

I met Pushpanath Krishnamurthy (Push), the activist and campaigner, when we worked together with Oxfam on the Make Trade Fair Campaign 20 years ago. His work to raise awareness around for fairer and sustainable alternatives to our economies and climate change, particularly for the most vulnerable, has been tireless. His long walks, are an example of this energy and passion.

This collection of encounters in Southern India over three months in 2024 is Push as the storyteller, and he weaves the stories that make up a tapestry of alternative local economies inspired by ancient crafts and wisdom, but with new purpose and meaning in the face of environmental and economic decline.

These are real-life stories of innovative nature-based, sustainable and regenerative economic alternatives that provide income for millions of people making organic coffee and foods, medical herbs, slow fashion and plant-based fabrics, wooden toys and papier mâché, waste management and recycling, hand-loom textiles with natural dyes.

As we look to the future, we need to find better ways to generate income and livelihoods that are sustainable and regenerative, adapted to the realities of climate change. And yet these economic alternatives, largely led by women, who have creatively perfected their crafts against all odds and obstacles, are "hidden beneath layers of invisibility, exploitation and disregard."

Push has an amazing ability to engage and connect with the people behind these stories, their lives and struggles, their faces and smiles, their hopes for the future, and he brings it to life with the sounds and colours, the flavours and rich aromas of the food and spices of India. It is a wholesome and inspiring collection of stories that give hope because of how they impact positively on people's lives and on the environment.

These are the sorts of stories behind the 200 Million Artisans initiative, which estimates that this number of people depend on crafts for their livelihood in India. How can a one trillion USD economy of 200 million people be "invisible" you might ask? Last year's Kula Conclave hosted by 200 Million Artisans facilitated connections between impact investors and entrepreneurs in India's creative manufacturing and handmade sector sought to raise awareness and visibility around this economy.

The Wellbeing Economy Alliance (WEAll) has supported these initiatives, because we see the importance of shifting the narrative around the economy, beyond growth and profits to wellbeing of people and planet, and we want to amplify the examples of flourishing alternatives that generate wellbeing.

Our economies and the economic and financial investment are still mainly driven by financial return, profit and growth margins, and these sorts of locally led initiatives which generate income and, more importantly, positive impact and wellbeing in people´s lives and the environment, remain underinvested.

This is why impact investment is so important. Can we really continue to invest in violent economies that destroy nature and people´s lives? Investors worry about risk, but the biggest risk to us all is not investing in these regenerative alternatives.

These stories help us see through the layers of invisibility and remind us that life is not a transaction, nor a return on investment. They help us see that behind every product is a story, a family, a community and our relationship with nature, and that there are positive, viable and non-violent alternatives.

Push tells these stories with characteristic humility as an ambassador for WEAll and Ahimsa. They are an invitation to open your eyes to another more hopeful but real world of alternative economies that can generate wellbeing and be in balance with nature.

– Simon Ticehurst
Wellbeing Economy Alliance

Introduction

"The reasonable man adapts himself to the world; the unreasonable one persists in trying to adapt the world to himself. Therefore, all progress depends on the unreasonable man." This line from George Bernard Shaw was pressed into my hands by my cerebral manager just as I was setting out from the cobbled streets of Oxford to the sweltering lanes of Bengaluru. The book was more than a gift; it was a manifesto for my work with the Centre for Social Markets in India—a guide for an unlikely adventure that would unearth the unreasonable in me.

The journey that followed was one defined by relentless curiosity and wild experimentation. We were determined to shake things up, crashing conferences with shameless opportunism, selecting studies at random, and seeing where chance would lead us. Out of this glorious chaos emerged *Made in Bangalore*, a book that began as a question: Can business be a force for good? It ended as a vibrant collection of stories, chronicling the work of fierce social entrepreneurs—those "unreasonable" people whose persistence was reshaping the world for the better. I had the privilege of leading this effort alongside a brilliant team, including the indomitable Viva Kermani.

It is 13 years after the above publication and in the the above context and specifically in the background of climate impact in India .I was exploring new business and enterprises that are based on past but in the art, craft, handloom and handmade sector that I came back to SouthIndia.

In the eight weeks that followed, traversing through South India in the heat of August, September, and October, I found myself immersed in a paradox. The weather was as erratic as the innovators I met—searing heat one day, unprecedented rain and thunderstorms the next, wild winds battering the countryside. And yet, everywhere I went, I met champions of India's handicraft and handloom ecosystems. These creators—stubborn, relentless, deeply rooted in tradition—were preserving ancient crafts while breathing new life into them. Their works weren't museum relics; they were living, breathing artifacts of Indian heritage, worn and used by people across the country and beyond.

Their world was a swirl of beguiling sarees, hypnotic blouses, and intricately crafted icons made from wood, metal, silk, and new-age vegan materials. Masters of their art, these artisans passed down their expertise to younger generations, mentoring apprentices in skills sponsored by both state and national governments. Their products, relying entirely on sustainable, nature-based practices, were largely the work of women—though men too had their place in this vast creative tapestry.

Consider the Prime Minister, recently seen in a silk shawl crafted from waste materials by a women's collective in Bhagalpur. It was a bold statement of intent from the government, signaling a desire to recapture the magic and markets of India's handicrafts and handlooms. This is an industry that accounts for $4.5 billion annually and employs around 10 million people—roughly 40% of Australia's population! It's the second-largest source of employment after agriculture in India.

And yet, it's the individuals who soldier on, despite immense hurdles, that truly stagger the imagination. Like the so-called Green Revolution that unchained India from its dependence on food imports, the handicraft sector has the potential to spark its own revolution—one that doesn't rely on toxic side effects or unsustainable practices. As K.L. Radharaman of the Angadi empire aptly put it, "The entire luxury goods industry of Europe traces its roots back to the craft guilds of the medieval age. India has that same potential to create a unique advantage, empowering a new generation of craftspeople and entrepreneurs in rural India. For those seeking an economic miracle, this is one success story hidden in plain sight."

Indeed, organizations **like 200 Million Artisans** argue that the handcrafted economy could grow into a trillion-dollar ecosystem, supporting 200 million artisans and craftspeople. Events like the **Kula Conclave**, which brings together stakeholders from all corners of the industry, are setting the stage for this fertile landscape of craft and creativity to flourish.

Here, amidst this rich tapestry of resilience, I'll capture just a glimpse—a distilled essence—of those valiant artisans who are, quite literally, reshaping the world one stitch, one carving, and one thread at a time.

Pulicat: The Salt Lagoon, Palm Leaf Baskets, and Mangrove Revitalization and the Kula Conclave 2024

Background: My journey has been intertwined with the Ahimsa economy, a movement devoted to the ideals of a non-violent, sustainable economy. In September 2022, I embarked on a nearly hundred-kilometer pilgrimage with men and women from across India and beyond. This odyssey led us to the heart of innovation, where stories were shared, and inspiration flowed freely among more than 180 artisans showcasing their handcrafted wares at a Santhai in Madurai.

For four days, we were cradled by the warmth of farmers and simple folk, who offered us shelter, food, and the comfort of sleeping on earthen floors. We were welcomed not just by individuals, but by the collective spirit of organic pioneers, housewives, students, and professionals. It was in this humble, yet profound gathering, at the first Ahimsa Santhai organized by CESI and others at the revered Gandhi Museum in Madurai, that we presented the concept of a historic Ahimsa path to then Finance Minister of Tamil Nadu, Dr. Palanivel Thiagarajan.

You may witness this journey in the film linked here.

What emerged from those four days of intense interaction—sessions with experts, activists, and thought leaders from across the globe, as well as dialogues with children and adults alike—was a deep sense of possibility. A promise, if you will, to forge a robust non-violent economy: one that is sustainable, climate-resilient, and capable of generating income while spurring innovation. It is an economy that embraces the concept of well-being as its core.

After much reflection, it was decided that this scattered but shared enterprise needed to be molded into a more coherent, vibrant, and promising economy. This vision required the establishment of a distinct brand—*AHIMSA*—underpinned by a cohesive code of ethics. Central to this vision was the need for active communication, interaction with others on a similar journey, and the bringing together of enlightened innovators, design experts, and investors to elevate the craft and handmade products economy.

Fortune smiled upon us as we connected with the WEALL economy movement. Through these conversations, we linked up with the magnificent *200 Million Artisans* initiative and the Kula Conclave 2. The *200 Million Artisans* project is a groundbreaking effort that highlights the immense power, significance, and extraordinary impact of handcrafted products—especially those created by women who often receive so little, yet bear the brunt of climate change, suffering its impacts first, worst, and hardest.

As a long time supporter of fairtrade and craft – and a climate Justice walker-I find this initiative original and substantial as well as realistic and affirmative-tuck in, Dip in, My freinds

https://www.kulaconclave.com/

Dip into the creative Kula platform-read, share, apply and be a part of this historic gathering with clear purpose.

To kick off the process for myself and

As always, my journey took me to the women who craft these products—to learn, understand, and narrate their stories.

Sixty kilometers from Chennai, in the village of Thiruvallur, lies Pulicat Lagoon, a place of breathtaking beauty and ecological wonder. Here, I met a handful of women on a blistering day, yet they toiled in a well-lit, airy, and congenial shelter under the auspices of the Pulicat Women Industrial Co-op, established in the 1960s.

The Palm Leaf Handicrafts produced here have earned a sterling reputation for their authenticity, creativity, and collective effort, reaching markets across the globe. There was a time when these products, with the support of institutions like the Commissioner for Handicrafts and associations such as South India Producers and Oxfam Bridge, found their niche. The women, who earned and learned much from this craft, saw it as a bonus to the main income derived from the lagoon's bounty—prawns, fish, and other natural products.

Pulicat Lagoon, the second-largest saltwater body, is a magical and biological marvel, its flora and fauna both incredible and overwhelming. Yet, the dual forces of human impact and climate change have dealt a devastating blow to the community that depends on this natural wealth. Life and livelihood are under significant threat.

Not long ago, a three-month harvest of prawns and fish would sustain a household for an entire year, with the earnings from Fair Trade baskets as an added bonus. But now, the economic decline is palpable. The scarcity of palm leaves—exacerbated by rampant deforestation, a shortage of climbers, and other factors—has driven up production costs.

Rita, Kokila, Zelka, Thaiba, Sakil, Safnia—women who collectively possess over 150 years of expertise, skill, and ambition—though battered, have not given up hope. They told me simply, "We need markets. Let there be new investors. But more importantly, we need additional training in new designs and processes." The baskets, soap holders, and other products they showed me left me in awe. Their needs were straightforward and solid. They weren't asking for charity; they sought partnership, investment, skill development, and new pathways to sustainable production—and, therefore, critical income.

During my visit, I also spent time with the remarkable Meerasa S., the founding member and managing trustee of the Mangrove Foundation. His work on mangrove restoration is a beacon of hope, offering multiple benefits, including a robust response to the climate crisis. This visit was profoundly significant for me—I learned so much, and felt deeply humbled by the courage and determination of the palm leaf basket-making women, alongside the pioneering efforts of Meerasa S., a child of the lagoon ecology and a champion of wetlands, recognized by the Government of India.

Learn more:

https://www.mangrovefoundationindia.com/about

On August 15, a day after our meeting, I learned that Meerasa had been awarded the Green Hero Medal by the Government of Tamil Nadu. He works closely with the palm leaf basket-making women who craft magical bamboo baskets and other items. Such intersections and cooperation are vital—just as vital as an event like Kula 2024! I hope a few of these women can attend Kula, and with the unwavering support of mentor Panjaksharan from SIPA, showcase their stories and connect with everyone in Goa.

As I left Pulicat – late evening-I saw a single Pink Flamingo – slightly away from its family forlorn and pensive-waiting.!

Please read share, comment and support-watch out for more stories in the next collections.

Leading a New Path by Application Creating Ahimsa Economy

Anantha Sayana: The name evokes a serene image—reclining one—but Anantha is anything but still. He is a whirlwind of activity, tirelessly working across different fronts: advocating for safe, healthy food while passionately spearheading the revival of hand-dyed, handmade clothing, recreated in vibrant designs that seem to bloom anew with every collection. His clothes beckon with ravishing colors, innovative cuts, and an allure that makes you want to try them all.

I first met Brother **Anantha Sayanan** in Madurai, though his two decades of impactful work had long preceded him. His speech at the Ahimsa Santhai in 2022 was nothing short of inspirational. He spoke with a rare combination of passion, knowledge, and authenticity—each word affirming a deeply held belief in sustainable living and community empowerment.

Our paths crossed again in Chennai, where Anantha and others were showcasing their work at a local fair. His own venture, Tula, was on display, but what struck me was his commitment to uplifting others alongside himself. He wasn't merely a producer; he was a facilitator, opening doors for fellow artisans, farmers, and creators.

Curiosity led me to his headquarters at the Organic Market in Indiranagar, where I found Anantha—affectionately called Anathoo—seated cross-legged on the floor, working through supply lists as his phone buzzed constantly with inquiries. Despite his busy schedule, he was generous with his time, walking me through the market, where each product had a story. As we moved among organic vegetables, dry millets, oils, grains, and medicinal herbs, Anantha narrated a saga of fifteen years of relentless effort. His work has given rise to over fifteen such stores—havens of wholesome, organic produce in a market otherwise dominated by crowded supermarkets.

His growing network of customers and volunteers trusts that, from seed to mouth, the products they buy are safe, fairly priced, and ecologically sustainable. Anantha told me how one senior IAS officer, deeply moved by his work, organized a talk that shifted government attitudes toward millets. No longer mere "bird feed," millets were being recognized for their potential to transform both agriculture and dietary habits. As the talk went on, senior officials were served multi-course millet-based meals, sparking both surprise and admiration.

As we continued our tour, **Anantha Sayanan** shared samples—a millet muffin, groundnut sweets, specialty chocolates—crafted by customers and volunteers. This wasn't just a store; it was a movement, themselves spoke of their authenticity. Sharp-eyed customers knew when they were getting if fake they spotted something fake, and quality always matched the price. Not fancy prices, but fair ones. The trust came not from external certifications but from the integrity of the product itself.

Scaling up, as Anantha sees it, is not about mega-stores but rather small, well-managed shops run by different generations of people, each contributing to a sustainable future.

For more on his inspiring journey, see this well-documented article: YourStory.

But what excites me even more is the story of handmade clothing and indigenous, sustainable dyes. Tula's range—filled with splendorous colors and innovative designs, crafted by design students and passionate supporters—is finding its footing in an industry otherwise ravaged by the negative impacts of fast fashion. Slowly but surely, Tula and its network are gaining traction. Engagement with stakeholders, consumers, schools, and producers is growing, and each item on the shelf carries a stunning backstory. Visit the store, and you'll feel it.

The organic movement is here, and it's thriving. We owe thanks to people like Anantha and his peers for their relentless efforts, for their refusal to give up in the face of exploitation, and for their steadfast belief in the power of sustainability. This two-decade journey is as complex as it is compelling, started by a handful of committed individuals who dared to challenge the system.

"I've never taken money from donors, trusts, or loans," Anantha said, "but tried a different path that works. Our scale, our certification, and our end users all know that this sustainable journey can be achieved—and must be—in this time of economic and ecological crisis."

A true champion of Ahimsa, I felt deeply humbled to meet and learn from him. When I asked if he would attend Kula 2024, he simply said, "There's no need for me to go. Others, who are looking for an investing path, might benefit. As for innovation," he added with a smile, "we've only revived what was always there."

For me, every step of his story is a path-breaking effort. In it, I see innovation, excellence, trust, confidence, and, most importantly, collectivity. It's the embodiment of a new Ahimsa economy, one that champions well-being.

In the coming days, I look forward to meeting some of the producers directly in Karnataka, Andhra Pradesh, and Tamil Nadu.

When a New Generation Redefines Business as a Force for Good Creating a Nonviolent Vegan Economy

"I had good days and very good days," said Joe Mitty, the erstwhile Oxfam shop manager known for his knack in selling anything, even a donkey tied outside the shop one fateful morning. It was a statement that lingered in memory, much like the encounters that unfold unexpectedly, resonating with profound significance.

Nineteen years ago, I had the privilege of meeting Joe, and his words have since woven themselves into the fabric of my thoughts. My recent meeting with Mahaveer Sandip Kumar brought Joe's words rushing back, as Sandip embodies a similar spirit of resilience and purpose.

Sandip, at thirty-nine, alongside his father, operates Sarita Sarees and Hand N yarns, a testament to their shared commitment to craftsmanship and sustainable living. For years, I passed by the signboard of an unusual "vegan silk" on my walks to Jeeva Park, silently promising myself to visit and understand more about this woman-led initiative(My assumption as one observes such inititive led by women but I was wrong in this case). It's been a journey marked by missed chances until now, prompted by my involvement with #KulaConclave and #200MillionArtisans, culminating in an encounter that struck a chord.

Meeting Sandip was the fifth such encounter, a pivotal moment that compelled me to pen this story. It's a tale of tumult and relentless pursuit—the journey towards making Ahimsa, non-violent enterprise, not just a vision but a tangible reality of immense worth.

Sandip greeted me with a gentle demeanor, yet his depth of knowledge and empathy for the craftspeople and communities resonated profoundly. His insights into the ancient crafts and the lives they sustain were nothing short of enlightening—a distillation of over fifteen years of unwavering dedication and understanding.

This experience, knowledge, commitment, passion and the pursuit of Ahimsa story is immense-what I write here is just the toplines.

"Hand N Yarns, is a vegan clothing brand," he explained, "born in November 2018 out of a mission to redefine fashion with compassion, offering an alternative to silk that respects all life forms."

Such a statement barely scratches the surface of Sudip's personal journey. He spoke of his roots in a thriving silk saree business inherited from his father, a fusion of Kanjeevaram and other regional silks. But his path diverged in his twenties, sparked by a profound stirring within him.

In pursuit of something beyond tradition and profit, Sudip embarked on a transformative journey, delving into Infinitism called Alma mater before, under T.T. Rangarajan's guidance. His father, witnessing the emotional upheaval, encouraged him to meet a traveling Jain monk Sri Pravin Jain in Chennai—a meeting that catalyzed Sudip's shift towards ethical, sustainable practices.

The encounter shattered his previous comfort with luxurious silks, replaced by a commitment to vegan silk and sustainable craft promotion as a way of life and business.

Sandip's travels across India unearthed myriad communities engaged in hand-printing, tie-dye, and other handmade crafts, each with its story of resilience and commitment to non-violent production. One such story, the Ikat artisans of Odisha, moved him deeply.

Known as "Bandhakala" or "Bandha," Ikat is not just a craft but a philosophy—a geographically tagged product since 2007, embodying a commitment to non-violence in every thread. Despite material poverty, these artisans embody a spiritual richness, adhering to Buddha's teachings in their production practices.

"This encounter," Sudip confided, "strengthens my resolve to promote non-violent, handcrafted clothing even more vigorously."

He is an exceptional recipient of certification from the organization – Beauty without Cruelty.

His business ecology is slowly having traction – his direct producers geta fair returns – interestingly, Tata foundation referes such hand craft communities to him for working.

The vegan silk business is both B to B as well as B to C.

Sandip offers a range – he does not impose his position but provides alternatives.

His gradual approach takes time, patient and constant effort but is finding traction.

A couple of key questions,I asked

WHAT ABOUT SUPPLY CHAIN MONITORING AND CLIMATE POSITIVE PROCESS:

Yes. Already we are deeply into this. As our sourcing is very strong and aligned to sustainability. This is going to become even more strong as we grow. And already all our production pattern is harming the environment on least basis.

Further, our production process is involving less carbon and water foot print compare to the machine based manufacturing. As we establish our concept we will try to reduce as much as possible.

Above working pattern is for B2B platform.

What next:

I want to take up veganism and sustainability on a global platform.

And want to create more fellowship who can take this concept for coming future times.

I am very eager to show the world that ethical and sustainable ways can still make a better living rather than just chasing money or fame. And for this I want to create an ethical business model which earns revenue at the same time saves the environment and create opportunites for the artisanal based society

As I bid farewell to Sandip and his team

In my book of life, Sandip Kumar is a master of innovation—a testament to the transformative power of embracing sustainable instincts and possibilities.

I sensed that the movement for Ahimsa and a well-being economy had found a champion and an excellent innovator and participant for Kula 2024

The Power of the Unreasonable People: Bengaluru

A short profile of people I met

Bengaluru, that swirling vortex of innovation and aspiration, where the unreasonable wield their power for change, beckons with tales of transformative visionaries. Among them stands Sree Ranga Rajan, the luminary behind Dibella India. Hailing from the arid lands of Ramnad, he rose through the rigors of textile studies in the UK to champion regenerative cotton and uplift smallholder growers organically.

Ranga, modest despite his immense expertise, graciously guided my first foray into Bengaluru's Initiatives for Development, a visionary trust steered by stalwarts like Salimath, a former banker, and a cohort of seasoned specialists in agriculture and enterprise finance. Together, we aim to bring regenerative practices and fair trade to North Karnataka, nurturing sustainability from grassroots up.

Amidst the city's pulsating rhythm, I found myself drawn to an exhibition of innovators, hosted by the Selco Foundation, where luminaries like Don Norman, sage of Everyday Design, shared insights with Bangaloreans hungry for transformative ideas. Negotiating the labyrinthine traffic, I arrived only to discover it was a private affair. Undeterred, my acquaintance with Harish Hande, founder of Selco, from our collaboration on 'Made in Bangalore,' bore fruit as he graciously showcased solar innovations powering everything from healthcare to honey dehydration.

The latter, a marvel by AltP Precision under Lakshman Sridhar's stewardship, mimics nature's finesse in drying honey using solar energy—a breakthrough poised for wider application, potentially transforming rural economies . The solar energy hospital – a Selco invention could transform energy deficit Zambia's country side and households .I was told WHO's thoughtful guidance with SELCO is in its way and hopefully Uka – impact pioneers can be part of such an initiative.

Yet, amidst these wonders, a meeting with Anil Annaiah, polymath and storyteller, stands out. His humility belies a breadth of achievements spanning literature to impactful films, each endeavor a testament to his commitment to societal good. Our impassioned exchange, spanning themes from health to social action, underscored his ethos of using intellect and wealth to bridge societal divides, encapsulated in his poignant words, "Health, intellect, wealth—the tripte issues defining global disparity."

Anil's upcoming venture, Sangoli Rayanna, promises to further this mission through art and activism, a beacon of hope in an increasingly complex world. His invitation to collaborate on Push-COP29, a social media initiative coinciding with the climate summit in Baku, is emblematic of his visionary spirit.

Unreasonable Champions: A Salute to Bengaluru's Fearless Citizens

I must confess that in my earlier reflections, I failed to mention a remarkable assembly of citizens from HSR Layout, Bengaluru—a group of relentless and unreasonable champions whose story deserves telling. Leading this battalion is the indomitable Dr. Shanthi Tmmala, a woman of fierce intelligence and compassion. A doctor by training, but by calling, a warrior for change, she left her medical practice behind to take on a battle of a different kind: the fight to reclaim a city buried under its own waste.

The once-proud Garden City had become a garbage city, its streets and parks drowning in the debris of unchecked urban sprawl. Solid waste, wet waste—it all piled up like a festering reminder of the cost of development without foresight. Waste management had become a nightmare, and the city, a grotesque parody of its former self. But where others saw disaster, Dr. Shanthi saw a call to arms. And in answering that call, she ignited a movement—mobilizing an extraordinary group of unreasonable residents, people who refused to accept the status quo.

Thus was born the *Swatcha Graha Kalika Kendra*—a beacon of hope in the heart of HSR Layout, a center dedicated to teaching the art of waste management and composting. What began as a small initiative soon spread like wildfire. Parks across HSR now manage their waste with pride and care, and a biodiversity park has sprung up, a living testament to the power of citizen action. The work of this movement is nothing short of contagious. Even a small group of awakened souls can transform a landscape—and the SGKK park is living proof, drawing visitors not just from Bengaluru, but from across the country and beyond.

Ratnakar Bhadravathi, a dear classmate of mine and a retired senior banker, recently reflected, "Dr. Shanthi is a living force." He is right, of course. Her energy is unflagging, and her mission goes beyond waste management. She champions menstrual hygiene, too—travelling to schools and colleges, spreading her message of awareness and dignity. Her influence has stretched far beyond Karnataka; this very week, she is working in Hyderabad.

"I couldn't ask for a better teacher than Dr. Shanthi," remarked a college student who visited the biodiversity park. And it's true—she is more than a leader; she is a force of nature. Whenever the chaos of Bengaluru—its suffocating traffic and towering garbage heaps—overwhelms me, I find myself returning to HSR Layout, where the likes of Dr. Shanthi, Ratnakar Bhadravathi, and other unyielding spirits remind me of the power of unreasonable action.

As I take the story of this citizen revolution from my home in Bengaluru to my new home in Cambridge, UK, I dream of connecting these remarkable leaders to my ward in Arbury, Cambridge South. Perhaps there, too, the flame of unreasonable action that is already in action will catch greater fire.

I salute these incredible citizen-leaders—individuals who took ownership of their surroundings and, by doing so, showed the world what it means to wield unreasonable power. I think back to the day I walked through the SGKK park, alongside students and adults, my dear friend Shiva Prakash among them. He had only come to seek advice on starting a nursery, but he was soon swept up in the fervor, chanting slogans for a plastic-free Bengaluru. It was then that I realized: with these champions leading the way, even the wildest dreams of change could become real.

As I reflect on these encounters, I eagerly anticipate sharing the next chapter of my journey—a rendezvous with Bhupathy, the visionary behind Chennapatna's eco-friendly toys, where innovation meets tradition in the pursuit of sustainable futures.

Toy Maker of Chennapatna

The unreasonable Toy maker-Shilpa Trust-Story

From the Wooden Toy Plains to the Coffee-Clad Mountains

The changemakers were on the move. Satish Parthasarthy—a vibrant, curious organic farmer, grounded in earth and code—and myself, carrying the hum of intent, set out with a mission. As always, it took an hour of wrestling through the urban labyrinth of Bengaluru's traffic—a place where time loses its meaning, and progress feels abstract—before the road finally untangled and opened like a sigh, revealing the motorway. And then, the landscape began to breathe.

Greenery everywhere, blurring into the horizon. Coconut groves swayed lazily, sugarcane fields whispered secrets, paddy swam in the air, and fruit crops punctuated the scene like quiet exclamations of life. The air had a softness to it, thick with possibility. We were headed towards the heart of something old and resilient: Chennapatna, the wooden toy town.

Seventy minutes later, we found ourselves in the shaded enclave of Shilpa Trust, greeted by the familiar sight of Bhupathy Madhavachary. Sleeveless muslin shirt, hands already deep in the wood that has carried his family's legacy for six generations. There he was, shaping toys that had journeyed from local markets to the far edges of the globe. His story—one of a child unschooled, a father bound by debt, and the slow, painful climb out of bonded labor—seemed like folklore, except it wasn't.

The weight of history clung to every word as Bhupathy spoke. His father's four-hundred-rupee debt, a lifetime tether to a wealthy farmer, hung heavy. The 1960s brought a sliver of hope—government initiatives, promises of revival—and for the first time, they glimpsed freedom. The boy, eleven years old, and his father, tired but resolute, began to carve their way out of bondage. Ten, fifteen-hour days working the land had given way to something else: toys. Delicate, intricate, sometimes as simple as bangles or wood necklaces, but they held the weight of freedom.

By 1985, the world had changed again. Fate, in the shape of a fair in Chennai, arrived. Panchaksharan—Panju to those who loved him—appeared like a character out of a fairy tale. He saw Bhupathy, saw the skill and soul behind the toys, and Shilpa Trust was born. A global supplier, certified fair trade. Bhupathy smiled gently as he recounted it all—learning English, navigating regulations, expanding horizons. "I learned so much," he said, the humility of a man who'd seen his world stretch and bend without ever breaking.

Satish, with his boundless curiosity, was in his element. He probed, asked, explored, while I wandered through the heart of Shilpa Trust—master craftsmen, women with hands as deft as time itself,

North Indian workers who arrived as apprentices and stayed as artisans. The place felt like a breathing organism, a vast, extended family where generational ties intertwined with the new. Women, fresh from government training, carved and polished with machines that sang of modernity. But the toys—oh, the toys—still carried that ancient magic in every curve and color.

As Satish and Bhupathy became animated, their conversation spun wild ideas—electric trains, alternative energy, solar-powered dreams. I couldn't help but smile. Here were two men, from different worlds, weaving a future that felt both audacious and inevitable. As we stood there, the scent of wood mingling with the hope of collaboration—coffee land meeting toy land—I realized this was more than a visit. It was a beginning.

Yet, behind Bhupathy's gentle smile, the scars of a brutal global economy lingered. The pandemic had ravaged markets, shaken the foundations he'd so carefully built. Shilpa Trust had weathered the storm, but it had left its mark. Now, Bhupathy's thirst was for more than survival. He spoke of diversifying, of reducing the carbon footprint, of partnerships that would honor both his legacy and the planet's fragile future. "We need markets, ideas, investors with a sustainability agenda," he said, his voice soft but clear. "But most of all, we need respect for our journey."

The words echoed in my mind as we left the toy town behind, driving toward the enchanting embrace of the Western Ghats. My heart swelled—full of gratitude for what we'd seen, for the connections we'd built, for the hope that was carrying us onward. Coffee land was waiting, as was the source of the Cauvery River. But here, in this moment, I felt the weight of stories unfolding, the beauty of something ancient yet new, and the gentle hum of change in the air.

While Western Ghats is in Peril – the Coffee Land Story Chiselling Many Paths

In the year 2003, my initial encounter with Sakleshpur's coffee growers and the Karnataka Growers Federation marked a pivotal moment. It coincided with Oxfam's impactful report, "Mugged," and a journey with Satish Parthasarathy, then in his late twenties, capturing the voices resonating amidst the global coffee crisis, particularly felt in Karnataka, Western Ghatts.

Without Oxfam's direct support, these resilient coffee growers rallied behind the "Make Trade Fair" campaign, amassing a staggering 200,000 signatures on locally crafted petition sheets, amplifying the outcry across the South. Dr. Pradeep's involvement with the Global Alliance of Coffee (GLAC) and subsequent adoption of the Common Code for Coffee (4Cs) further underscored their commitment.

By 2009, although Oxfam had shifted focus, my ties with the Western Ghats remained steadfast — the vital lungs of the South and the master regulator of India's monsoons. Oxfam's pivot towards climate discourse in 2009 led me on a transformative journey to Copenhagen, igniting my affiliation with the Center for Social Markets in Bengaluru and rekindling my connection to the Western Ghats.

The ensuing "Coffee to Go?" study became a watershed moment, illuminating the intertwined fates of South Indian coffee, grown under a triple canopy, and the imperative of sustainable Arabica cultivation in preserving the Western Ghats' rich biodiversity. This collaborative effort with stakeholders became a hallmark, echoed by robust reports from the Hassan branch of the Coffee Growers Association, documenting challenges, innovations, and the enchanting diversity of flora and fauna.

Fuelled by my passion for coffee amidst global trade turbulence and mounting climate threats, the community faces uncertainties: soaring production costs, volatile prices, and relentless bouts of disease and disaster. Yet, amidst these adversities, the growers remain proactive. Initiatives in natural and organic farming, diversification, value addition, and international certifications are forging new pathways.

It is inspiring are the "Seven Bean Team," a cadre of young and middle-aged farmers employing cutting-edge techniques to optimize yields and minimize ecological footprint. Despite their success, challenges persist: from climate shifts and market volatility to labor shortages.

Yet, the Western Ghats' fragile ecosystem remains a pivotal lifeline, sustaining monsoons and livelihoods alike.

In my encounters with Asha Shvaprasad and Nadita Das of the Women Coffee Promotion Council, dynamic entrepreneurs forging a path in coffee production, I glimpsed resilience and innovation. Their journey, spanning a quarter-century, epitomizes the region's vibrancy and the evolving plantation economy's trials.

Lastly,noteworthy among these efforts are the Arehally farmers, guided by veteran activist Raje Gowda, alongside newcomers like Satish and Priya, blending modern expertise with traditional wisdom on their modest 3-acre plot. Certified organic and marketing through innovative channels, these pioneers offer a beacon of hope. Their organic practices mitigate climate impacts, enhance biodiversity, and ensure sustainable livelihoods, all while yielding promising returns. Vikas,the Son of Mr Raje Gowda joins the company of Priya to set a blazing path fully regenerative and eco friendly business partnership.

As we confront these multifaceted challenges, the urgency of safeguarding the Western Ghats grows clearer. Its biodiversity and ecological vibrancy are not mere luxuries but essential to sustaining life and livelihoods. With optimism, I entrust the future to the burgeoning youth brigade, already taking strides to address these complexities.

The story of Coffee Land unfolds not just as a tale of cultivation but as a testament to resilience, innovation, and the delicate balance between tradition and modernity. Watch this space as the narrative continues to evolve.

Unreasonable Innovator of Belagavi

Poornima Jagtap:

In the timeless words of George Bernard Shaw, "The reasonable man adapts himself to the world; the unreasonable one persists in trying to adapt the world to himself. Therefore, all progress depends on the unreasonable man." It is this unyielding spirit, the defiance against the stream of conventionality, that courses through the veins of Belagavi and Guledgudda, places where the unreasonable have carved their destinies with rugged determination.

The journey from Bengaluru to Belagavi, aboard the slow chugging night train, was marked not by slumber but by a state of restless anticipation. Sleep eluded me, perhaps owing to the incessant screeching brakes and the rhythmic departures and arrivals of nameless passengers. A peculiar thing, that—the act of briefly sharing a space with strangers, a flicker of life passing by in the dark of the night, only for them to be swallowed up by some distant station. As dawn crept in, so did the landscape—vivid green fields unfurled, crops swaying to the breeze, as the train gained altitude and Belagavi drew nearer. Thirty years—it had been that long since my last visit, and the city, like many others, had swelled unpredictably in size, but not without its own idiosyncratic rhythm.

I awaited Poornima Jagtap, an indomitable force, the kind of person Shaw would describe as "unreasonable." Her truth, etched into every action, is a battle cry against life's odds, fought with creativity and integrity. My mouth, parched from the night, had hoped for a simple cup of tea from the station café, but it seemed even that was denied—change was scarce, no tea. But as soon as I reached Poornima's home, that small deprivation melted away into a flood of warmth—a cup of chai, thick, aromatic, paired with soft potato-stuffed rotis. Here, at last, was sustenance. Gathered around her were others, including the familiar face of Gopikrishna and a fellow intern, young and eager, ready to learn.

Quickly, we made our way to Sainagar, to a house where Poornima was building something miraculous—a rooftop space for women, diverse in caste and faith, yet united in their hunger to learn, to create, to earn. The house stood on what was once a lowland, a place that grew rice and sugarcane, but now prone to flooding. Much like the women's lives, the soil had endured its share of trials. Power looms hummed in some homes; in others, handlooms were remnants of a fading tradition. COVID-19 had brought economic devastation, and floods had exacerbated the suffering. But amidst all that anguish, there was hope. The women, eager and shy, began to show us their work—crochet samples, sarees, textiles—delicate, vibrant, alive with promise. One by one, their hands unfolded stories of resilience, of defiance against the cruel whims of fate. Fatima, cloaked in her hijab, spread her creations before us—a quiet revolution in thread and wool.

In Poornima, I saw a vision blossoming. She had founded the Agastya Foundation, along with a small shop, Warsaa, where the handmade products of these women would find buyers, not out of charity, but because they were extraordinary. In that space, I encountered another force of nature—Robert Edward Lloyd. Once a designer to Bollywood's elite and Dubai's royalty, Edward had turned his back on the high life, choosing instead to channel his talent into empowering the women of Belagavi. He arrived after a nine-hour train journey, yet his spirits were undimmed, his humor intact. Holding a purse designed by the women, he gently remarked, "Simply superb," his hands gesturing with the grace of a dancer. And then, as if it were nothing, he sketched three designs—luxurious, affordable, elegant. His heart burned for a commission from the Kula campaign, but Poornima, ever the strategist, resisted. "I'll go to Kula next year," she said, her voice ringing with conviction. The unreasonable woman, determined to bend the world to her will.

The Unreasonable Handloom Fighter of Guledgudda

In the timeless words of George Bernard Shaw, "The reasonable man adapts himself to the world; the unreasonable one persists in trying to adapt the world to himself. Therefore, all progress depends on the unreasonable man." It is this unyielding spirit, this defiance against the flow of convention, that pulses through the very heart of Belagavi and Guledgudda—two places where the unreasonable have carved their destinies with raw, unrelenting determination.

Guledgudda

A town, if it could be called that, cradled among rocky hills like an ancient secret. The roads here—if they could be called roads—are snaking paths barely wide enough for two souls to pass each other without brushing elbows, squeezed between rows of houses where the incessant clatter of power looms drowns all other sound. That noise, that relentless hum of industry, bounces off the boulders that stand sentinel, weathered by centuries of wind and rain, as if nature herself has grown tired of fighting and decided to let the town and its people thrive in this rocky embrace.

We left early, before dawn had fully awakened, to escape the snarls of traffic that choke Belagavi, the second capital of Karnataka, a city over a thousand years old. Belagavi is a place where history and modernity battle for supremacy—a strategic military and trade hub, perched on a high plateau, yet falling victim to the chaotic embrace of unchecked growth. Here, buildings spring up like mushrooms, and the city hums with the energy of its youthful, bustling population, always in a hurry to be somewhere.

After hours on the road, through dust and heat, we found ourselves at the foot of the hills, finally relieved to see the "Gudda." Guledgudda—a name that echoes with the footsteps of migrants, artisans who came here, each bringing with them their crafts, their trades, their stories. It's a town where art and life are woven together as tightly as the threads of the famous Khana weave.

Guided by the grace of smartphones and the kindness of strangers, we met RameshAyodi, a man whose face lit up with a shy, yet welcoming smile. He led us through the maze of narrow lanes to his home, where his wife Amritha and a few young workers were busy mending, packing, and cataloging the vibrant Ilkal saris, their colors so rich they seemed to pulse with life. These saris, carried from the hands of local weavers, some on handlooms, others on powerlooms, are as old as the land itself, their designs a living link to the past.

But Guledgudda is known for more than just the Ilkal sari. It is the cradle of the Khana weave, a design at least four centuries old, inspired by nature, and by the intricate carvings of the ancient temples of nearby Badami, where the Chalukya dynasty once ruled. The Ilkal saris, with their natural dyes, their history stretching back a thousand years, once saw indigo bricks transported on hand carts, an unimaginable sight today.

It's here that Ramesh's story begins, a man in his late twenties, who, like many dreamers, envisioned a life far removed from the loom. "I wanted to pursue a technical course," he said, his voice tinged with nostalgia, "a great job, a house, a car, a life of comfort." But the reality was harsh—he couldn't afford it. Then came the government's offer of a diploma in textiles and handicrafts, with a stipend that would cover his needs. That decision, he says with a smile, "changed my destiny."

Before that, Ramesh had never seen a loom, never touched cotton or silk, or even polyester. But during his course, he became immersed in the world of textiles, learning the craft from seed to fabric, from the earth to the loom. He found himself enchanted by the mystery, the magic, the sheer artistry of it all, as though the ancient art had seeped into his very soul like a soft breeze, leaving him forever changed.,

His first assignment took him to **Charaka** a handloom center nestled in the Western Ghats. Isolated but beautiful, the village was surrounded by green mountains and flowing rivers, a landscape that seemed pulled from the pages of myth. The natural beauty, the rich biodiversity—it all worked its magic on Ramesh. Charaka became his muse, his sanctuary. "I owe everything to Charaka," he says. "And to Mr. Prasanna. That's why I named my son after him." He blinked away tears as he spoke.

When COVID struck, it was nearly the end. Business dried up, and the once steady stream of orders for saris and blouse pieces slowed to a trickle. Friends helped him through the worst, but people who see Ramesh today have no idea of the struggles he faced—the moves, the sacrifices, the dreams deferred. He still dreams of a larger space for his work, a place with more light, more room for creativity to flow. "I'll pursue it," he says, that same shy smile playing on his lips.

In a town where handlooms once stood on the verge of extinction, threatened by powerlooms and cheap polyester, Ramesh has breathed new life into the Khana weave. His vision is to transform this ancient craft into a luxury product, a symbol of both tradition and innovation. His creative diaries, bound in Khana fabric, have become a hit—a small, colorful testament to his ability to adapt and survive in an ever-changing world.

Each diary is as unique as the person who will eventually write in it, infused with the energy of the artisan who crafted it, the two-toned vibrancy of the fabric giving it life. The patterns, the motifs—they seem to whisper stories of their own, waiting for new ones to be written.

Ramesh has done more than revive a craft; he has revived a community. He has brought back over 150 weavers from the brink of despair. There was a time when they considered burning their looms, throwing them into the Holi bonfires—a symbolic gesture of their frustration, their surrender to a world that no longer valued their art.

But Ramesh, with his unreasonable spirit, has turned the tide. He dreams of a Guledgudda where the looms hum once more, where the streets are alive with the vibrant colors of Khana cloth, where creativity and sustainability walk hand in hand. As Poornima packed 40 saris and diaries for the Mysore festival, I couldn't help but feel a swell of joy. Ramesh—a new-age migrant with an ancient soul—has the power to transform this rocky town into something extraordinary. Much more in the spirit,like many of the previous migrants-the Guleds.!

Though climate change both directly impacting the weavers – the heat for one is so severe-and the weavers women, and men – have to cut down the hours they can work and times hands blistering.

Besides the cost of yarn to transporation and competion from synthetic fakes is mounting but you can never kill the zest for revival and lust for reimagination for a better and sustainable life.

And Guledgudda will rise again, its looms singing songs of triumph and thrive.

Be a part of the transformation:

https://www.khanaweaves.in/the-story

The Unreasonable Hero – Enigmatic Artist in Belgavi

The enigma of Shiva: Artist and the living fire

Then there was Shiva Ranjan—a fisherman turned wool artist, whose long, untamed tresses and quiet intensity spoke of a mind deep in contemplation, yet ablaze with creativity. Son of Vital and Savithri, he narrated his story in a measured cadence, each word a drop of wisdom. His father, a lover of all creatures in the forest, a snake catcher, a man of the earth. His mother, a fisherwoman, whose dowry had been paid in sheep. Perhaps it was through those sheep that Shiva had absorbed the soul of his art. His latest creation, a sprawling woolen canvas woven from Deccani sheep's wool, captured the essence of the shepherds he had lived with, their stories of survival etched into each fiber.

"Everything is connected," Shiva whispered, almost to himself, as his eyes traced the contours of his work. His connection to nature, to the stories passed down through generations, flowed into his art. His gaze turned serious, "Climate is impacting the Deccani sheep, the shepherds. I want to color that truth." His work, he insisted, must not only capture the beauty of life but also ensure that the shepherds benefit from the art they inspired. "I am still evolving," he admitted, a shy smile breaking his intensity.

In his masterpiece, a cosmic tapestry of shepherd life, I saw the world reflected back in swirling wool—yet something felt missing. The women, I thought, their untold stories still waiting to emerge. I kept that thought to myself, unsure if it would unleash the volcano of passion buried within his calm exterior.

In Belagavi, Guledgudda, and places like them, unreasonable people—people like Poornima, Edward, and Shiva—refuse to accept the world as it is. They push, they pull, they create. They progress. And it is in their unreasonable defiance that the future, perhaps, is born.

The Unreasonable Hero of Hydrabad-Sudha Rani Mullapudi

In the grand tapestry of the handcraft ecosystem, many threads—both big and small—are woven together by an intricate supply chain. From artists who sell their creations directly to those whose work reaches buyers through various intermediaries, the stakeholders are as varied as the crafts themselves. In Karnataka and Bengaluru, I have chronicled the lives of many such heroes—those who embody the spirit of a singular or multiple roles within the craft world. Some are creators, some are sellers, others are enablers, and a few take on the mantle of nurturers. Among them, rare are the super designers who harmonize all roles to preserve, promote, and add new dimensions to these ancient arts.

Yet there are a few—unreasonable in the best sense of the word—who go beyond mere passion. They possess an unwavering knowledge, skill, and dedication to handlooms and crafts. They not only preserve these traditions but also breathe new life into them, transforming themselves into artful custodians and savvy promoters. One such enabler is Sudha Rani Mullapudi.

Sudha is someone with whom I share the honor of having worked with at Oxfam, though our paths had not crossed in person until one fateful Sunday when I, along with Sivaramakrishna, finally met her. I had followed her career trajectory for years, admiring her journey from afar, but meeting her in person was something else entirely. Rarely does one encounter a person who has transitioned from a career in development aid to dedicating their life to the revival, promotion, and sale of handloom and handicraft products. Sudha's story is extraordinary because she herself is singular, incomparable—a true original at every stage of her life.

One of the earliest women graduates in horticulture, and likely the first female postgraduate from the National School of Agribusiness, Sudha's journey began with her foray into rural development, where she spent two decades learning, building, innovating, and contributing. From her varied responsibilities in development to her later passion for handlooms, Sudha has always moved with purpose. So, when she dived into the world of handlooms 15 years ago—leading programs on market access, heading Tradecraft, and eventually founding her own social enterprise, Abhihara—it was a natural extension of her lifelong commitment to fairness, sustainability, and innovation.

Abhihara, which means "the ability to rise against difficult odds," is an enterprise that nurtures cotton, handloom, and crafts from Telangana. Here, the stories of cotton, craft, and handloom intersect to breathe new life into ancient traditions, painting them in the vivid hues of magic, justice, and audacity. To Sudha, this audacity is second nature. "Though we struggle with unfair competition from mill products, unregistered players on social media, rising raw material costs, high overheads like stall rents, transport costs, and the burden of GST squeezing our margins, I never felt like giving up. I believe we will sail through," she said with a spark of defiance.

https://www.abhihaara.com/

And sail through she did. When the pandemic crushed small businesses, Sudha's ability to build a network of supporters became her armor. With the goodwill she had nurtured over the years, Sudha not only survived but flourished, innovating her way forward. That's the thing about Sudha—her mind is always at work, inventing.

On that Sunday, despite her many responsibilities, she made time to meet us. She was late, but that delay worked in our favor, as it gave us time to locate her office, nestled on the first floor of a nondescript building on a street filled with the humdrum architecture of squeezed apartments. Sudhakar Bandaru, her gentle but formidable deputy, spotted us wandering and guided us inside with a smile and a call from the window. A glass of water, a cup of tea, and we were welcomed into an atmosphere filled with slow, thoughtful conversations.

Sudha arrived, radiating energy and joy, wrapped in a magnificent red handloom saree. Apologizing for her tardiness, she launched into her story—an incredible journey marked by personal loss, professional obstacles, and the unique struggles of a first-generation woman entrepreneur who was determined to go beyond profit, to share revenue fairly, support heritage, and sustain an entire ecosystem. She smiled while recounting moments that would have left others in tears. When she spoke of her latest innovations—"We've started making Gollabhama khadi sarees using natural dyes and also zero-zari Gadwal cotton sarees using three shuttles"—her face lit up, and it was as if the stacked sarees and displayed crafts around us had come alive, dancing in vivid colors and joyful rhythms.

For over three hours, we listened to her stories, asked questions, and shared in her anguish and triumphs. I asked her if there was a single moment that made her rethink, reimagine, and bounce back from the bruises life had dealt her. She paused, reflective. "There are so many," she said, "but if I had to pick one, it would be when I was one of five women entrepreneurs invited to the Global Entrepreneur Summit in 2017." Her eyes glistened with pride.

Dr. Sivaramakrishna, who normally would have added many thoughtful observations, was uncharacteristically quiet, simply smiling with a happy admiration. "What a story," he murmured.

Before we said our goodbyes, I was thrilled when Sudha agreed to apply for the innovation competition at the Kula Conclave. She had also graciously arranged for us to meet handloom weavers and metalcraft artisans in Pochampally the following day. As we left, Bernard Shaw's famous quote about the "unreasonable person" bringing about real change came to mind. Sudha is the embodiment of that energy—authentic, innovative, and full of integrity. She is not just reviving a precious heritage; she is shimmering it with newfound magic.

When I asked her what does all this struggle and breakthroughs means

"Though we are struggling with unfair competition from mill products too many unregistered players on social media etc increasing raw material costs high over heads like stall rents stock transport,GST which is a burden and squeezing our margins never felt like giving up and has the belief that we will sail through"

She has more than sailed through – a true inspiration and nurturer.

Her story, and the stories of those like her, prove that the vast potential of India's handloom and handicraft industries—often touted as a trillion-dollar economy with enormous employment potential—can only be realized with the vision and courage of individuals like Sudha Rani Mullapudi.

The Unreasonable Extrordinary Activist, Anthropoligist and Linguist of Hydrabad

Tomorrow, the curtains will rise on the Kula Conclave in Goa—a visionary initiative by 200 million artisans determined to reshape the narrative of craft and creativity. This moment feels like the crescendo of a symphony I've been writing for weeks, chronicling the unsung heroes of unreasonable art, resilient craft, and the timeless traditions of handloom.

https://www.kulaconclave.com/

My journey, spanning four South Indian states, led me to the beating hearts of these artisans. Each encounter felt like unearthing a rare gem—stories of extraordinary transformation, of weathering relentless storms, both figurative and literal. These creators, despite the cruel weight of climate change, breathe new life into their art with boundless imagination, tenacity, and the sheer will to reimagine.

Among them, Dr. Sivaramakrishna's story stands as a radiant finale, the perfect epilogue to this odyssey of rediscovery. His work unveils a sacred tapestry, interwoven with the art, craft, and culture of indigenous peoples, each thread an ode to their profound bond with the natural world.

Here is the celebration of revival and resilience, where the intimate dance between humanity and nature becomes a testament to survival, beauty, and hope. Read on, and let these tales awaken your own sense of wonder.

Founder: Dr. Sivarama Krishna

"The British model would have us think that the Tribal is the antagonist in the pursuit of forest conservation." – Dr. Sivarama Krishna, Founder of SAKTI

In 1985, Dr. Sivarama Krishna established SAKTI (Search for Action and Knowledge for Tribal Initiative), an NGO born from a deep understanding of tribal knowledge systems. A decade before, he had earned his doctorate from Osmania University in 1982 for his pioneering work on "Tribal Knowledge Systems," a field he would later champion. In 1987, Sarada Devi, who became his wife, joined him in this journey of service and advocacy for the tribal communities of India.

Dr. Sivarama Krishna's doctoral thesis was a unique contribution to anthropology and linguistics, rooted in a vision that foresaw the integral role of tribal communities in both preserving and managing forests. "The candidate has chosen a topical subject, very relevant to our thinking on culture, cognition, and language. His linguistic and anthropological reasoning is sound. His language is clear and simple." – Report of external examiner Prof. A. Munirathanam Reddy, S.V. University, Tirupati, December 6, 1982.

When I first met Siva in 1985, I was struck by the symbolism of his name. It bore the weight of great mythological figures — powerful, triumphant, yet burdened with responsibility. But what seemed an immense legacy was a mantle he wore with a quiet, determined grace. Siva's resolve was unmatched, and it was this very resolve that led him to dedicate his life to uncovering the hidden wisdom of the tribal communities, their symbiotic relationship with forests, and their deep-rooted ecological knowledge. Far from being outsiders, the tribals are, as Siva would often say, part of the forest, part of the ecosystem.

Siva's childhood was far from comfortable or secure. His father, a wandering minstrel, sang songs of Lord Krishna in the villages, while his elder brother supported Siva's education through sheer grit and determination. Few from their socio-economic class make it as far as Siva did, especially to earn a PhD — a feat that continues to inspire many. Despite the allure of academic prestige or environmental fame, Siva chose a path of hardship, not popularity. For over three decades, through struggle, rejection, and apathy, he has held steadfast to one core belief: that tribals, armed with an understanding of law, due process, and administrative frameworks, can challenge the system and claim their rights.

Siva's work is not just about activism or policy reform — it's about respect. Respect for the knowledge, practices, and wisdom of the tribals. His work teaches us that we must understand and respect indigenous cultures, for in their harmony with nature lies the blueprint for a sustainable future. What Siva and SAKTI have done is not simply a fight for rights, but a battle for recognition of the rich contributions of tribal communities to environmental conservation and sustainable living and the rich art, craft and culture they represent

Siva's Journey and Vision

Though Siva could have easily found a teaching position in a tribal school, it was through that very experience that he discovered his true purpose. He saw the profound connection between the tribals and the forests, a relationship not just of survival, but of reverence, sustainability, and symbiosis. It was a life dedicated to self-sufficiency, mutual respect, and ecological balance. Siva realized that the forces of politics and economics, not the tribes themselves, were the ones disrupting their way of life. The forest, which had once been their lifeline, was being ravaged — its wealth misused by external forces. But armed with knowledge of the law and a deep understanding of tribal culture, Siva knew that the tribals could reclaim their rights and protect their heritage.

I recall walking with him through the lush hills of Gudem, as he recited poems that captured the essence of the Konda Reddy tribe's life — their culture, their connection with the land, and their unwavering determination. Siva, with his large feet and infectious laughter, became my guide. I was a stranger to this landscape, but he shared with me his vast, almost encyclopedic knowledge of the tribes of the Godavari region. At that moment, I knew Siva was more than an academic or an activist — he was a living bridge to the wisdom of the land, a mentor in every sense.

His work at SAKTI began with something simple: an audit of tribal skills and knowledge, culture and crafts. But it became much more than that. It grew into an enduring effort to empower tribals not only with knowledge of their rights but also with the tools to navigate the world of governance. Siva's work would go on to prove that genuine change comes not from radical ideology but from recognizing and strengthening what is already there — the tribals' rich heritage, of art, poetry, crafts and their understanding of the forest, their profound connection to the earth.

Siva's work has never been about seeking accolades or recognition; it's about practical, sustainable solutions. Through legal petitions, advocacy, and relentless community building, SAKTI has secured crucial rights for the tribals — from fishing rights in Rasul Cheruvu to recognizing Chenchu villages as revenue villages. But more than that, SAKTI has breathed life into the very idea of "empowerment" by ensuring that tribal knowledge and culture are preserved, recognized, and honored.

A Vision for the Future

Siva's dream for the future is as ambitious as it is profound. In 2008, the government proposed transforming SAKTI's office in Rampachodavaram into a Tribal Knowledge Park. Although the project faced setbacks, Siva's vision remains clear. The revitalized park will serve as a hub for tribal culture and knowledge, integrating traditional wisdom with modern technology. This will not just be a place for learning; it will be a space where the past and present meet, where young tribal communities can reconnect with their roots and, in doing so, protect the future.

As Siva shared with me his plans to geo-tag tribal knowledge systems and create a digital archive of tribal crafts and practices, I realized the depth of his vision. This was not just about preserving the past but about ensuring that future generations could access and understand the rich heritage of India's indigenous peoples.

In the face of global climate change, the world needs the knowledge of the tribals, the art, the craft, the stories and poems more than ever. The delicate balance they maintain with nature is a model for sustainability in a time of environmental crisis. The work of SAKTI and Siva is a beacon of hope, showing us how to protect our forests, our environment, and our indigenous communities and the rich tapestry of the cultural and artistic expressions. in a way that is holistic and just.

Conclusion: A Legacy to Support

Over the last three decades, Siva has never wavered in his commitment to the tribals. He has empowered them, not just to survive, but to thrive. And in doing so, he has shown the world that true empowerment comes not from charity, but from respect and collaboration.

His work has not been easy, but it has been revolutionary. His success is a testament to what can be achieved when we listen to those who have always been in harmony with the earth. His life's work is a treasure trove of lessons for anyone who cares about the environment, indigenous rights, and social justice.

Now, as we look to the future, Siva's mission continues. His vision for a Tribal Knowledge Park is just one of the many milestones in a journey that has already achieved so much. But the road ahead is long, and it is up to us to ensure that this vision comes to life. Will you join me in supporting this magnificent effort?

Siva – for me after meeting so many unreasonable powerful change maker – embodies the full extent of what Bernard Shaw had in his mind when he wrote that the unreasonable one is and will be the source for changing the world.

The perfect unreasonable one.!

Siva's journey is far from over. And it is a journey we must all take — for the sake of our planet, our people, and our future.

I was reading, quite by accident, at that moment, the biography of the legendary environmentalist, Dr. Madhav Gadgil. It was an uncanny coincidence, for it made me realize—after having spent three intense days with Siva and observing the intricacies of his organic journey spanning over three decades—that he too deserves a biography. Siva, with his quiet yet profound contributions to the world, would never write such a book about himself. His focus is on the paths he treads, the programs he nurtures, the plans he's still forging in the quiet spaces of his mind.

But it is clear now: we must do it, not for him, but for the present and future generations.

In the cosmic tapestry of the tribes, where time coils in its own rhythm and the universe itself hums a song of ancient power, there unfolds a world that is both vast and intimate. Here, in the fold of the earth's green embrace, lies the rich artistry of life: the vibrant hues of craft, the eloquent echoes of poetry, the stories woven from the breath of the wind. These are not mere expressions, but living testaments to the deep, unspoken knowledge that each tribe carries—knowledge of every inch of the forest they inhabit, every leaf that unfurls, every whisper of the earth beneath their feet. Their wisdom, inscribed not in books but in the pulse of the land, is a map of life's delicate balance. It is a universe where every being, from the smallest insect to the tallest tree, is woven into the same sacred fabric, each living with purpose, each playing a part in the endless dance of creation. They know the forest like they know the beating of their hearts—its secret rhythms, its quiet breaths, its vast, living soul. Here, in this world of intricate beauty, there is no separation between the land and the people. They are one, existing in a cosmic harmony that stretches across time and space, a testament to the wisdom of a people who have never forgotten their place in the universe.

There's a wider, urgent need for his story to be told—not as a matter of self-promotion, but as a legacy that will echo across time, a roadmap for others to follow. The story of Siva is not just his own, but a reflection of the wider, pressing call to preserve and protect our world. It must be written, for it is not merely his life that stands as a testament, but the hopes of all who will inherit the earth after him.

In ensuring the wellbeing of the planet, we safeguard the vitality of its inhabitants, for the health of the earth is intricately woven with the fate of all who dwell upon it.

The Unreasonable Champions of Handcarft from Telengana

The Unreasonable Pochampalli Weavers and the Pembarti Metal Magicians

Escaping the snarling chaos of Hyderabad traffic, we slipped toward Pochampalli, greeted by a quiet, drowsy town stirring to life in the golden dawn. The rugged landscape stretched out as we drove—a theatre of stone hills, ancient forts silhouetted in the distance, goats grazing, and women lining the roads, seeking daily work. Pockets of greenery and shimmering ponds punctuated the otherwise arid terrain, the gift of an unruly, short-lived rainstorm that had flooded Hyderabad just days before.

Pochampalli—more than a town, a fabric of history and resilience, caught in the warp and weft of its people's hands and dreams. Known for its iconic Ikat sarees, this town, nestled in the warm-humid zone of Telangana's Yadadri Bhuvanagiri district, also bears the name "Bhoodan" after Vinoba Bhave's land-gift movement, where voluntary land redistribution was envisioned but left in skewed ownership patterns across this dry, unforgiving land. Here, weaving isn't merely a trade but a lifeline, with power looms threatening to overtake the delicate art of Ikat—a technique where patterns are dyed onto yarn before weaving. Yet amidst this modern encroachment, small green shoots of revival began to sprout, nurturing a new vision for handlooms.

Our hosts, Lakshman and his spirited wife, Sharada, emerged from the morning mist—anything but the sleepy figures one might expect in such a place. Lakshman quickly orchestrated visits to homes where traditional weaving had found new expression, a revival born of stubborn resilience and a glimmer of hope. In their airy new home, built with wide-open spaces for looms, Lakshman and Sharada spoke of hard-won achievements and unyielding determination. Sudha and Abhinara had provided much-needed support, a lifeline in the tempestuous waves of the pandemic that swept over them. Stockpiled sarees languished, unsold, as bank interest mounted and despair knocked at their door. But Sharada, teary yet resolute, clung to faith in this craft, to the colors and textures that still held the possibility of transformation.

From Lakshman's, we ventured to meet **Shankar and his wife Lalitha**, who welcomed us with unbounded warmth. Shankar, fresh from receiving accolades, held a silk saree in his hands, one that had taken months to create—a masterpiece displayed before the President of India. His passion for plant-based dyes and handlooms seemed to transcend the physical, a near-spiritual calling to harmonize art with nature. His brother, a power-loom operator, watched skeptically from across the street, dismissing Shankar's craft as impractical. Yet as students from a local design college gathered to learn from him, it was clear Shankar was more than a craftsman; he was a guru, his pink Pochampalli shirt a badge of quiet rebellion against convention, his home a sanctuary of preservation.

Our journey continued toward Pembarti, the metalwork town, winding past the Musi river as it swelled with rain-fed vigor. A roadside dhaba offered us sustenance, its humble fare of roti and dhal unexpectedly exquisite, nourishing us for the path ahead. Pembarti, known for brass artifacts, hummed with industry but bore signs of a town caught between old and new—garish new constructions fueled by city-dwelling relatives' remittances stood side-by-side with the traditional cottages of its craftsmen.

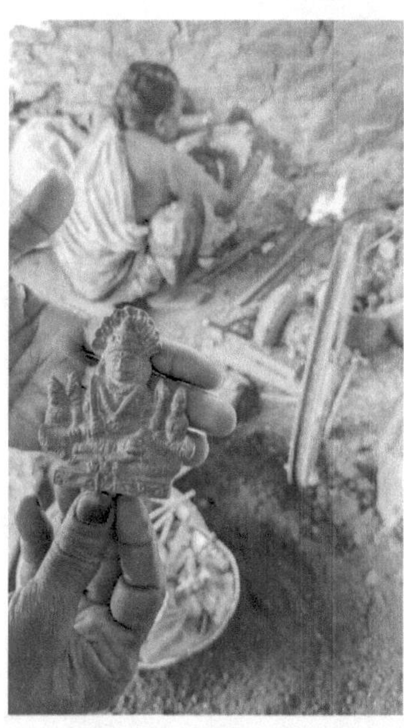

Our visit brought us to Narasamma, a diminutive, quietly proud widow who single-handedly sustained the craft her husband had taught her, working in a charred backyard that served as her forge. Her deft hands, small and weathered, stoked the flames, handled molten metal, and poured it into casts with a calm fury. Her movements were swift and sure, her craftsmanship unflinching despite the sweltering heat. As the final shape of a deity emerged from the embers, Narasamma allowed herself a rare, fleeting smile—a moment of pride and accomplishment that left us awed. She shared her struggles, her isolation, the indignities she bore as a widow—yet here she was, resiliently carving out a living, her artistry a testament to her fortitude.

Narasamma's parting left us humbled, in silent reflection as we retraced our route back to Hyderabad's damp, rain-soaked streets. Her words echoed Hannah Arendt's insight that "one deed, one word, can change every constellation." In Narasamma and her forge, in Shankar and his handlooms, we glimpsed a new constellation of hope—unreasonable, and utterly tenacious.

The Unreasonable Handcrafters of Pondicherry

The Invisibly Unreasonable Pondicherry Handcrafters

Pondicherry is a place where art and craft pulse through the streets like the very lifeblood of the city. Amid the hustle and bustle, there are countless artisans – skilled, independent creators who labor quietly, often without recognition, their stories hidden beneath layers of invisibility, exploitation, and disregard. Yet, despite the weight of these burdens, they continue to shine, creating handcrafts and handloom products that are not only compellingly beautiful but also rich in heritage and sustainability. These are the unsung heroes, those who are self-employed, yet whose creations have the potential to transform the economy, offering jobs and hope with the simplest of supports and a modicum of respect.

It was not the usual bustling markets I sought, but something deeper. I wanted to meet two artisans working in the government-supported Craft Village at the edge of the city. Our driver navigated the sweltering midday traffic with a practiced ease, and, just when I thought we might never make it, we arrived. There, nestled within a sprawling space of well-constructed shops and winding walkways, the atmosphere was a delicate balance between anticipation and quiet expectation. The Craft Bazaar, a testament to the government's support for small-scale individual artisans, was slowly waking up to a trickle of customers.

At every corner, I was captured by the astonishing variety of products—earth, coconut, leather, wood, and even upcycled plastic—all formed into something new, something vibrant. The sheer artistry on display was mind-boggling. But it was at Shop No. 7, tucked away on a corner, that we encountered Shiva Perumal, a man whose very name carried the weight of the Hindu Trinity. Shiva, however, was anything but divine in his bearing. Small and quiet, he shrank into himself, smiling shyly but speaking little. His silence was thick, almost impenetrable. Yet, with Uma, my wife, an artist herself, by my side, we slowly found a way into his world.

Shiva's story, unfolding in halting words, was one of struggle and survival. Born in Pondicherry, the only son among five children, his father—a daily wage laborer—earned a mere 100 rupees a month. Poverty was a constant companion, and survival was not just an option, but a way of life. As a child, Shiva worked alongside his father, making plastic ropes for hours on end. His education, cut short after the tenth grade, became a casualty of necessity, as he needed to earn for his family. Yet, despite the hardships, his spirit remained unbroken.

Shiva's memory of an early traumatic experience—being thrown into a sewer by a drunken man, his clothes stained with filth, only to be punished at home for it—marked him for life. He vowed never to drink anything other than water. Perhaps it was this trauma, this humiliation, that fueled his determination to rise above the circumstances, to create something beyond the shackles of poverty.

Shiva's journey took him to a shoe factory, where he worked for a time, before he found his true calling in paper mache. Initially an office boy in a lamp-shade making workshop, Shiva absorbed every detail of the craft, eventually becoming a bookkeeper. In 1996, he had his big break, working with a Frenchman in Auroville. "It was my lifetime break," he recalled with a shy smile. From office boy to maker of paper mache creations, Shiva found immense pride in the fact that his handmade items were bought by foreigners and sold abroad.

Now, with a shop of his own, Shiva has weathered many storms. The pandemic nearly broke him, but thanks to Anita Canaga's support, he was able to keep his craft alive. His latest creation—an exquisitely crafted diary made from recycled paper and cloth—was a testament to his dedication. "I spent six weeks perfecting it," he said, gently cradling the book. There was a humble pride in his voice, a quiet celebration of his accomplishments.

The shop itself was a visual feast, filled with products that bore Shiva's unmistakable stamp of authenticity and creativity. Everything was priced modestly, with the hope that his artistry would be recognized, that his creations would not only support him but also create opportunities for others. Shiva's story is one of resilience—a man who has faced unimaginable hardship, yet refuses to give in. He dreams of a day when his craft, and the craft of his fellow artisans, will receive the recognition and support they deserve.

But Shiva is not alone. At the other end of the Craft Village, we met Theresa Mary, another remarkable artisan. A graduate in Tamil, Theresa hails from Karikal, and like Shiva, she never imagined she would one day become a craftswoman. "Good fate led me here," she said with a confident smile.

Theresa's journey into the world of palm leaf craft began when, at the age of 27, she was selected for a government program that paid her a stipend of 750 rupees a month. It was a small beginning, but it gave her the training she needed to create her own products. COVID-19, however, threw her life into disarray. With a large stock of unsold items and her husband losing his job, the economic impact was devastating. But Theresa was undeterred. She found a way to move to Pondicherry, where she rented a small space in the Craft Village, and slowly, her confidence in her craft grew.

Now, despite challenges like rising costs and the unpredictability of the market, Theresa continues to create. Her designs, mixing palm leaf and upcycled plastic, have gained attention, and she remains determined. "Though uncertain, my designs are attracting people," she said proudly. "We have overcome much, and we will continue to do so."

What gives her the most joy is when the local government asked her to share her knowledge with design students. "I knew I had arrived," she said, her eyes sparkling with pride. Theresa's ambition is clear—help us with the market, she urged, and we will show the way for ourselves and others.

It was these two artisans, Shiva and Theresa, whose stories of perseverance, resilience, and quiet creativity moved us deeply. They are the embodiment of what it means to be a part of an invisible, unreasonable force—craft warriors whose work sustains not only themselves but their communities. They are the true champions of change in a world that often overlooks the power of handcrafted products.

As I left the Craft Village, I was filled with hope. The future, I believe, belongs to these small, unsung handcrafters—their work is a bridge between heritage and sustainability, a living testament to the quiet revolution happening in the world of Indian craftsmanship.

All the artisans have the skills and I want as much as possible to collaborate with them to create some new high end products . Their work should be recognised and valued by people which is missing in the current world. People buy designers products without bargaining but when it comes to artisans handcrafted products people bargain and find them expensive.

The Unreasonable Aurovilian

Uma and the Spirit of Upasana

Uma, the unreasonable Aurovilian, (life long member of Auroville international community at South India – www.Auroville.org)

She call herself embodies the essence of this paradoxical truth. She is the force that disrupts convention, bends the rigid structures of expectation, and paves a new path for those who follow. She does not simply adapt to the world; she remakes it, stitch by stitch, story by story, from the humblest of threads to the vastest of dreams.

Her life is a mosaic of contradictions that weave together into a singular, transformative narrative. Silent and introspective, she can slip into a trance, her gaze distant as though tracing ancient lines in the air. And then, suddenly, she erupts with the kind of gleam in her eye that speaks of a story—something ancient yet entirely new. A tale from a forgotten time, or a vision of a world that could be. When she speaks, it's like the rhythm of breath itself: gentle, warm, hospitable, yet potent, always carrying the weight of an entire cosmos. She is that center of gravity for wandering souls— young, old, or somewhere in between—who come to her, seeking both sanctuary and purpose. She nurtures them, nourishes their dreams, and sends them forth with the knowledge that they are part of something far larger than themselves.

But who is this extraordinary woman? Uma Prajapati is, in many ways, an enigma wrapped in the fabric of the world. A "pocket rocket," as one might call her, she has redefined the notion of entrepreneurship. She is a thought leader, a creative activist, a traveling salesperson for conscious clothing, and a force of nature who believes in business with a soul.

She comes from a small historic town, Gaya in Bihar, humble yet stable—a conventional upbringing with its prescribed routines and modest comforts. But Uma, even as a child, could never quite conform to the boundaries of small-town life. She was always looking beyond, through the four walls, to the infinite possibilities outside. Her studies were excellent, but it was the lens through which she saw the world—of joy, creation, and subtle rebellion against the status quo—that set her apart.

When she ventured into NIFT Delhi in 1991for design education, the transition from a small-town girl to a metropolitan student was not easy. Shyness, self-doubt, and the weight of being the "only" often clouded her early days. But Uma was no ordinary woman. She topped her class, rising from the shadows of her insecurities to make waves in a world that had yet to understand her. An exceptional job followed, the kind that promised comfort and security. But Uma, never one to rest on her laurels, quickly grew disillusioned. The conventional path no longer held any allure. And so, she left.

It was a serendipitous encounter at an Auroville stall in trade fair in Delhi that opened a new chapter in her life—a meeting that transcended mere coincidence and signaled the convergence of her creativity and spiritual aspirations. For the next two and half decades, she would embark on a profound journey of self-discovery, of growth, and of becoming something far greater than she ever imagined.

The sacred trifecta of The Mother, and Shakti is at the core of her essence. Uma dreams of reaching for the stars, but her feet are firmly grounded in the values of fairness, femininity, and sustainability. "I am a businesswoman, but I also carry the energy of the Earth," she smiles, her voice a soft echo of the sacred teachings she holds dear.

Her work, like a great river with many tributaries, weaves through three interconnected streams: Upasaana, Rohini, and Tsunamika—each a vital part of her journey, each one contributing to the greater narrative of change.

Upasana—the foundational tree of Uma's work—symbolizes the fusion of creativity and spirituality. Derived from the ancient Vedic tradition, Upasana refers to devotion, worship, and the act of meditative connection with the divine. It is not just a clothing brand, but a living, breathing ecosystem that carries within it the principles of veneration, organic production, and sustainability. Each garment, whether organic khadi sourced from within India or a uniquely designed piece, holds deep reverence for the environment, for the hands that make them, and for the communities they support. From thread to cloth to garment, the focus is always on nurturing, honouring, and celebrating life in all its forms.

Uma's brand is not just about fashion—it is a quiet revolution. Her products, sold through Auroville and Pondicherry, bear certification from Fairtrade and the World Fair Organization (WFTF), but her true pride lies in the way these garments weave connections—from organic cotton farmers to weavers, from yarn makers to artisans. Pricing, though higher than mainstream fashion, is always fair, always conscious of the people behind each piece.

But Uma's impact doesn't stop at the market. Through Upasana, she creates a space for young seekers—those who come to Auroville from every corner of the world, yearning to find a deeper meaning in their lives. She guides them, teaches them, and ensures that they become part of the very ecosystem of sustainability she so fiercely nurtures.

Then there is Tsunamika—a handmade doll crafted from waste clothes, a symbol of the ocean goddess, born from the devastation of the 2004 tsunami. She is not for sale. She does not follow the rules of commerce. Instead, Tsunamika exists to tell a story. She is the voice of the ocean, reminding us of the fragile balance between our actions and the planet's wellbeing. Her creation has led Uma to global recognition, with Tsunamika becoming a symbol for ocean conservation and the protection of marine life. It is not just a product; it is a call to action—a powerful narrative about the regeneration that can arise from destruction. Tsunamika's impact is both local and global, having found a home in the hearts of people worldwide, sparking conversations about sustainability, climate change, and the urgent need to protect the oceans.

Finally, Rohini, the sacred house of life and nourishment, embodies Uma's vision of hospitality and care. It is a space where people come to learn, to grow, to heal—a nurturing womb that shelters those on a path of self-discovery. Through Rohini, Uma offers not just a physical shelter, but an emotional and spiritual refuge. It is here that visitors find solace, whether they are seeking solace from the world's chaos or simply hoping to find their next step in the journey of self-realization.

In conclusion, Uma's journey is not one that can be easily summed up—it is an ongoing evolution, a force of life that flows in many directions, touching countless lives. She has become a thought leader, an advocate for sustainability, and a global ambassador for the protection of the ocean, weaving together design, spirituality, and social activism in a way that no one else has before.

When I first met Uma in 2015, she quietly redirected my climate walk towards Auroville. That night, I stayed in Rohini, surrounded by a community of people from all walks of life. It was a profound experience, one that stayed with me, just as Uma's work continues to stay with all those she touches.

It sounds like Uma's journey of education and personal growth has been both transformative and inspiring. When she first began her education outside her home, she faced the challenges of navigating an unfamiliar path, one that lacked clear guidance or structure. However, through her resilience, creativity, and determination, she managed to not only pave a way for herself but also create a path for others to follow.

This story illustrates the power of self-determination and innovation. Uma didn't wait for an ideal or established route; instead, she forged her own. Her journey serves as a beacon for others, showing that even in the absence of a clear path, one can create new opportunities and systems that benefit the community. A true unreasonable leader.

Today, nine years later, I am honored to swim in the world of Tsunamika and to share in the cosmic journey that Uma has so courageously embraced. Her work is a testament to the power of the unreasonable—those who refuse to accept the world as it is and instead, create something far more extraordinary in its place.

I am grateful. I am inspired. And I am changed

The Unreasonable Slow Fashion Path Breaker of Tamil Nadu

The fantastic unreasonable recreator of slow fashion: TamilNadu

In the eight weeks traversing through South India in the heat of August, September and October, I found myself immersed in a paradox. The weather was as erratic as the innovators I met—searing heat one day, unprecedented rain and thunderstorms the next, wild winds battering the countryside. And yet, everywhere I went, I met champions of India's handicraft and handloom ecosystems. These creators—stubborn, relentless, deeply rooted in tradition—were preserving ancient crafts while breathing new life into them. Their works weren't museum relics; they were living, breathing artefacts of Indian heritage, worn and used by people across the country and beyond.

Sowmya Van Baaren embodies the real spirit of the unreasonable change maker – creating an ecology, economics, inclusive and innovative path.

This is her story-real Hibiscus hero.

In the soft amber light of an Auroville afternoon, as my eight-week odyssey across the subcontinent's artisanal heartlands drew to a close, I felt drawn to the last bastion of my journey—Pondicherry and more importantly Auroville. It was Uma Prajapathi herself, the visionary force behind UPASANA, who beckoned me to the oasis of Auroville, a fertile ground where dreamers, designers, and doers converge to reimagine sustainable living.

We began with Kalki's showroom, where the air hummed with the silent vibrancy of plant-based fabrics, every stitch and seam whispering the narrative of hands and hearts behind it. Standing there, surrounded by the scent of organic cotton, and the tactile pleasure of handmade, I felt transported—ushered into an era of elegance and grace rooted in the earth. There, amidst the custom-crocheted designs and cuts as fluid as nature itself, enchantment gripped me; each garment seemed to breathe with life.

Just as we were soaking in this wonder, a surprising invitation came: Sowmya, the brand head, with a smile as warm as the day, appeared with an unexpected offer, "Come, visit our workshop." There was no ceremony—only the openness of this place that held within it the quiet spirit of transformation.

We arrived early at the workshop, my wife—a writer, poet, and artist by her own right—joining me for the first time on one of these journeys. Waiting for our hosts, I was struck by the names of the brands—*Hibiscus Heroes, Two Be Two*—each one brimming with meaning, rich with the fire of intent. "Hibiscus Heroes," especially, resonated with me, a harmonious collaboration between two extraordinary women, Sowmya and Anyuta, embodying the timeless spirit of creativity and the bold vision of sustainability in garments that hold the earth close.

The atmosphere in the reception was serene, the air scented with the aroma of freshly brewed coffee, flowers, and earth. There, Sowmya and Anyuta shared their tale, one of colors coaxed from plants, leaves, flowers, and roots—a palette both ancient and new, a story of cloth and care intertwined. When beneficial purity, embodied in Sowmya's name, meets grace, held by Anyuta, something truly powerful emerges—a transformative force, organic and alive, a testament to the world they want to build.

In 2015, on a journey through the textile heartlands of Tamil Nadu, Sowmya's vision sharpened. Walking alongside the sacred river Cauvery, now sullied, she felt an urgent calling. "The river was dark, poisoned. If people have worn clothes since time immemorial, then how did we once manage to live in harmony with nature?" That moment of dissonance planted the seed of *Hibiscus Heroes*, a return to the heritage of natural dyes, plant-based fabrics, and the pursuit of a new way forward in clothing.

Today, *Hibiscus Heroes* is a flourishing expression of slow, mindful fashion. Sowmya, a young mother then, gave up the glitz of global fast fashion to bring alive a collection dyed by the hands of nature itself—clothing that tells a story, one bound by tradition yet modern in its appeal. Every garment a dialogue, every shade a memory of flowers and leaves.

At their workshop, we watched the workers—mostly women from local villages—confident and skilled, each engaged in a craft that feels both old and new. The process was meticulous, slow and deliberate, a commitment to quality that transcends profit. In their eyes,

I saw the pride of artisanship, a reminder of what is possible when creation is more than a transaction, when it becomes communion.

In their words and work, a vision materialized—an economy of well-being, as attuned to the spirit as to the cloth itself. The garments—crafted from organic cotton and plant-based fibers—speak to more than just style. They are a reclamation, a rebellion against the harm of fast fashion, a testament to resilience, renewal, and the enduring beauty of a world rooted in harmony.

Here was someone so deeply in tune with both the material and spiritual worlds—knowledgeable yet humble, always open to learning and sharing. This woman believed that one beautiful hibiscus was never enough; they felt a profound need to support and be part of a larger movement dedicated to creating, promoting, and scaling a sustainable, well-being-centered economy, where outer and inner growth happen in tandem.

Sowmya envisions *Hibiscua* as a sanctuary of knowledge, a luminous crucible where skills are not just taught but lived. This centre of excellence, named for the resilient hibiscus, is more than a school—it's a stirring testament to craft, resilience, and reverence for the earth. Here, the next generations of visionaries, designers, and sustainable entrepreneurs will find a practical haven where ideas are nurtured with both rigor and tenderness. They will work with their hands and hearts, learning the old ways while daring to create new ones, so that *Hibiscua* becomes both a place of becoming and a legacy for the world.

I had goosebumps—I could clearly see how this energy, vision, and reality are not only viable and possible but urgently needed.

As I walked out of that space, my new Hibiscus shirt warming me against the heat of TamilNadu, I felt a sense of protection—a soft armor from the earth herself. It wasn't just a garment. It was a story, a heritage, and a quiet revolution that I was proud to wear, as much a statement of self as of the earth beneath our feet.

Learnings that are precious

A pollution-free, biodiversity-rich South India—lush, tropical and in many ways a reservoir of ancient practices—holds an irreplaceable value. Scattered throughout are a few rare, authentic craftsmen, the keepers of knowledge and techniques that teeter on the brink of extinction. Many hesitate to share their wisdom, resistant to any influence that might dilute or commodify their craft, yet there are those willing to trust.

In understanding the craft and its materials, the truth is undeniable: while chemical and industrial processes are scalable and cost-effective, they wreak havoc on nature and on the laborers bound to them. Workers endure debilitating health issues, while plants and natural dyes offer a benign alternative, sparing the ecosystem and often possessing medicinal qualities themselves. This approach, rooted in ancient wisdom, offers benefits on all fronts—physical, psychological, spiritual and financial.

The inherited palette of natural resources might appear limited, yet it's abundant with possibilities. Our great-grandmothers worked within similar constraints, innovating and reimagining with what they had. With today's eco-friendly technology, this tradition can be expanded to rival even the largest commercial brands. But this journey demands due diligence. Responsible sourcing is paramount, as opportunists and exploiters lurk, eager to profit at any cost.

South India's bioregions hold more than enough resources, provided they are conserved and wisely shared. But no resource taken should come at the expense of food security or ecosystem balance. More than ever, this work requires a supportive community—peers aligned with our values. Equally important is building a body of consumers who understand and cherish the novelty and deeper meaning of the Hibiscus brand.

Partnerships with researchers and academic institutions can expand our impact, drawing in students, interns, and fresh minds eager to contribute. As our story unfolds, it must be told—boldly, broadly, with passion. The world needs to know we exist, to engage with us, to join in our journey. Much like the Kula 2024,200million artisans, we are part of a larger movement of 200 million artisans redefining what craft and commerce mean.

Patrons are essential, new ones who can nurture and sustain our vision. Authenticity, diversity, and creativity in form will be our hallmarks, possibly requiring self-certification to uphold standards and a collective voice to influence policy and practice.

Looking forward, the future belongs to the "Hibiscus Heroes": a centre of excellence that amasses a rich body of knowledge and skills, serving as a launchpad for a new generation. This center will cultivate young pioneers who, understanding the intrinsic value of this work, will carry it forward with resilience and innovation, forming a new cohort of craftsmen, designers and changemakers.

The Bounce-Back Queen: Anjali Schiavina – The Unreasonable Transformer of Pondicherry

It was an unremarkably hot afternoon in Chennai when Pondicherry first entered my orbit—not the Pondicherry of heritage postcards or glossy travel brochures, but an entirely different Pondicherry, one that breathed innovation and boldness. That Pondicherry belonged to Anjali Schiavina.

The call came from Abhishek Jain, the CEO of Fairtrade International India. "Can you come to Bangalore? You must meet Anjali," he said, the urgency of his tone implying that this wasn't just another meeting. She had returned from Istanbul after attending the Fairtrade Towns Conference and meeting Bruce Crowther, the concept's visionary founder.

As someone who had worked with Oxfam and Fairtrade long before it became a European certification powerhouse, my interest was piqued. Fairtrade wasn't just an idea to me—it was a journey I had been part of for decades, connecting the dots between South Indian producers, handloom weavers, and global ethical markets. When I met Anjali in Bangalore, her energy was palpable, her ideas audacious. And so began a friendship that would redefine how Fairtrade could manifest in India.

Anjali Schiavina: The Mandala Spirit

Born in Calcutta and raised in Auroville, Anjali's life embodies the dual spirits of her two homes: the intentional, ecologically driven community of Auroville and the vibrant cultural cauldron of Pondicherry. These twin geographies are more than a backdrop; they are the very fabric of her life, infusing her with an energy and inventiveness that has left ripples across the worlds of ethical fashion, sustainable enterprise, and community development.

In 2002, Anjali founded Mandala Apparels Pvt. Ltd., a venture that began humbly with a vegetable-dyeing unit, a tailor, a master cutter, and eight handloom weavers. Within a decade, it grew to a 165-employee enterprise with a global footprint. The company name, "Mandala," was no accident. In its radial symmetry, it reflected Anjali's vision: an interconnected enterprise where every thread—

from ethical sourcing to sustainable manufacturing—was part of a greater whole.

Mandala was more than a business. It was a bold experiment in sustainable fashion and community empowerment, providing hundreds of women their first taste of economic independence, skills, and self-confidence. For Anjali, Mandala wasn't just about garments; it was about weaving a future where ethics and economics could co-exist harmoniously.

But growth is a double-edged sword, and Mandala's meteoric rise attracted challenges that undermined its stability. Vested interests and rapid expansion took their toll, leaving Anjali at a crossroads.

Rising from the Ashes

For most people, the collapse of a dream like Mandala would be final—a narrative of despair. But Anjali, the unreasonable transformer, thrives not in straight lines but in the zigzag of struggle, reinvention, and breakthrough.

She made an extraordinary promise to herself: "I will pay everyone fairly. I will honor my commitments." And that she did, despite the years of effort it took.

Simultaneously, Anjali threw herself into a new mission: spearheading the Fairtrade Towns movement in India. From initiating discussions in nine cities to publishing a handbook on Fairtrade Towns, her work culminated in the first-ever Fairtrade Towns conference in India, held in Pondicherry in 2021. The event, meticulously curated, garnered global attention and showcased Anjali's ability to build communities that transcended geographies.

The Sea Beckons

One might have thought Anjali would finally rest, sip her Fairtrade tea, and reflect on her achievements. But true to her nature, she dove headfirst into a new adventure. This time, it was the sea.

Along with her husband, an environmental campaigner and sea-surfing enthusiast, Anjali co-founded the Pondicherry Yacht Club. The initiative is more than a yacht club—it is a celebration of the ocean, a gateway for locals and visitors alike to experience the Bay of Bengal's beauty and fury.

The Yacht Club is not just about sailing; it hosts monthly music events, showcases Pondicherry's rich art and craft heritage, and serves as a platform for ecological awareness, especially around issues like marine plastic and overfishing.

Anjali, with her characteristic modesty and meticulousness, has ensured that every detail—from safety protocols to the club's affordability—aligns with her ethos of inclusivity and sustainability.

The Mandala Reimagined

Whether walking through Pondicherry's cobbled streets or riding its windswept seas, Anjali Schiavina remains a force of nature, a human mandala radiating resilience and possibility.

Her journey has not been a linear wave of success. It has been a tumultuous dance of struggle, failure, and transformation. Yet, through it all, she has remained true to her core: an unreasonable changemaker who dares to dream big and uplifts those around her.

Anjali is more than a pioneer; she is a lesson in how to ride the unpredictable waves of life—how to transform ashes into fertile ground, despair into hope, and a local vision into a global movement.

As I bid goodbye to this extraordinary woman after a weekend at her impeccably curated Airbnb, my heart swelled with gratitude. In a world obsessed with success as a straight line, Anjali Schiavina stands as a testament to the beauty of the imperfect mandala, its every curve and color a story of perseverance, innovation, and boundless generosity.

Concluding Reflection

Each of these extraordinary stories, as distinct as our individual fingerprints, holds profound lessons. Rooted in specific contexts, they reveal a deeper connection to heritage, yet each entrepreneur navigates the present-day compulsions with a keen awareness. Sustainability, a core value for all, meets the formidable force of market dynamics, driving innovations from raw material procurement to product design, attuned to local, national, and global needs.

It brings together generations: the older, wiser women sharing their insights with their family of daughters and daughters-in-law, while the grandfather imparts his wisdom to his son, bridging the past with the future. This fusion of past and future is reimagined and recreated in every sense, weaving together a tapestry of tradition and innovation, where each thread tells a story of resilience and continuity.

Central to their ethos is a passion for the authenticity of their materials and products, coupled with a readiness to embrace new ideas, seek partnerships, and attract investment. These narratives transcend mere entrepreneurial success; they are poignant life lessons for aspiring businesspersons.

Moreover, they offer invaluable insights for policymakers, urging them to craft frameworks that support such ventures. For consumers, these stories advocate sustainable consumption and the transformative power of ethical purchasing decisions. Investors, too, find an enticing opportunity in ventures that balance profit with sustainability.

To policymakers, these stories present a pathway to economic revitalization, job creation, and environmental stewardship in the face of climate challenges. The diverse profiles of these changemakers—from different geographies, genders, ages, and educational backgrounds—underscore the potential of the arts, crafts, and handloom sectors to drive innovation, economic growth, and ecological resilience.

Despite myriad challenges, these entrepreneurs have not only started but thrived. Their success underscores the potential for greater achievements with appropriate policies, practices, and investments.

India, emerging as a powerhouse in this sector, signifies not a sunset economy but a beacon of new dawn—a sunrise powerhouse poised to lead in sustainable development – A formidble Ahimsa/wellbeing economy that grows and provides unique and practical possibilities for all life.